Bethany

A Story Worth Telling

A Story Worth Telling

J. Kimberly Cartis

ISBN 9781687273222

Edited by Kristin McCue

To my children,

Life is full of struggle, heartbreak, and mistakes, but overcoming
adversity
is one of life's greatest gifts. Hold on to this truth.
I love each of you with my whole heart.

Love,
Mom

Author's Note

Many of my conversations with Grandmom have taken place at the kitchen table where I learned bits and pieces of her story over many years. One of my favorite pastimes is to drink tea together and talk about life. I broke a sacred family custom because I don't like traditional Japanese green tea—I prefer Lipton black tea with sugar. Grandmom doesn't care, she fixes me the green tea anyway. But I never mind, because another fascinating story is always just beyond the next sip.

シブヤ.セツ子

SHI buYA Setsuko

Jennifer

Table of Contents

Prologue

2002

I'm 17 years old, and I'm sitting on the bed with Grandmom. We relax and chit-chat using a comfortable mixture of Japanese and English. My limited Japanese flows more easily when I'm around her. Away from her, I can barely recall any words in Japanese at all. Granddad refused to allow anything other than English in the house when Mom was growing up, so she missed out on the opportunity to be fluent. I'm sure he had his reasons. Mom and I try our best to learn what we can. Despite being in the United States longer than she lived in Japan, Grandmom's English is still very limited.

My name is Jennifer, but that is too difficult for her to pronounce. Instead, she calls me "Kimechan" from my middle name, Kimberly.

Grandmom rubs my legs with lotion like she's done a hundred times on my visits growing up. Suddenly, her eyes grow distant and sad. "Kimechan, I had hard life." She looks at my legs. She tugs her pants up to her knees so I can look at hers. "Grandmom not take bath for two years during war," she says in her broken English. She makes a fist and knocks on her calf. "My legs hard like turtle shell. I no have shoes. I walk two years in mountains. My feet like stone. Not look human." The last words were almost a whisper.

I can see the pain in her eyes, and I know the storytelling is over for now. I don't say a word. I grab the lotion and begin massaging her legs to comfort her.

Part 1

Setsuko

Without darkness we wouldn't notice the light.
Without sickness we wouldn't appreciate health.
Without evil we wouldn't understand kindness.
Without suffering we wouldn't know what love is.
Without pain, there would be no healing.
Without problems, we would never experience the happiness of solutions.
Without villains, there could be no heroes.
Without failures, we would never know triumphs.
Without death, life would be arbitrary.

It's their opposites that give meaning to our words, not the word itself.

—J. Kimberly Cartis

Chapter 1

1923

On September 1, 1923, a 7.9 earthquake hit Tokyo, Japan around noon. A mother was cooking in her kitchen. She felt the tremors and understood what was about to happen. Japanese people are no strangers to the fear of earthquakes. She screamed at her older children to *run*. Then she searched for her nine-month old baby, who had just been crawling around the floor. She spotted a foot. Frantically, she grabbed the baby by the ankle, and ran for her life.

It wasn't until she reached the bamboo trees that she realized her baby was slightly purple. The baby had been hanging upside down while she ran for safety. She shushed and comforted the screaming, scared infant. "It's okay, baby. We'll be safe here in the bamboo trees," she soothed. Japanese people know the flexible roots will keep the bamboo trees from snapping.

Suddenly, the trees shook violently. The mother heard screaming from the city. Not everyone made it to safety.

An estimated 140,000 people died that day in Tokyo, Japan.

That baby was my grandmom.

The Early Years

Setsuko Shibuya was born in Japan on January 3, 1923. She was the third of eight children and the eldest daughter. She was famous for being the ringleader. An independent spirit and mischievous child who hated school, she told me how she would go to her neighbor's house and steal watermelons. She and her sisters would play hooky from school and go to the beach. Watermelons can float. They used them as flotation devices when they swam, then ate them for lunch.

Chapter 2

1940

As was the custom in Japan, Setsuko's marriage was arranged when she was five years old. She got married at 17 and went to live with her husband in China. He lived in the northeast corner of a region called Manchuria, which was occupied by the Japanese at the time. Her husband and mother-in-law owned a restaurant in a city near the Khingan Mountains.

Setsuko was young and felt so alone with these people she'd never even met before. She was in a foreign country and didn't speak Chinese. Not long after the marriage, Setsuko ran away and went home to her family in Japan. It took her four days to travel there by train and boat. When she finally arrived home, she discovered that her arrival had been preceded by a telegram from her mother-in-law alerting her family that she had run away. Setsuko's mother allowed her to stay only three days and then forced her to return to her husband.

Soon her husband began going to geisha houses and running around with other women. Her mother-in-law blamed Setsuko, saying that she was a bad wife and that's why her husband wouldn't come home. Setsuko despised her mother-in-law, who abused her.

Setsuko ran away twice more. Each time her parents made her return to China. Things got so bad, she became desperate and ran away to another city in China by herself and began waitressing to earn money. At first, the owner of the restaurant was nice to her. He bought her new clothes. But it wasn't long before he started demanding sexual favors in return. Setsuko escaped. Starving and penniless, she was forced to return to her husband.

Chapter 3

1941-1942

On December 7, 1941, Japanese planes attacked Pearl Harbor at 7:55 AM, annihilating most of the U.S. Navy fleet. More than 2,400 Americans died that day. On December 8, the United States declared war on Japan.

Six months after the attack on Pearl Harbor, the United States defeated the Japanese in one of the most decisive battles of World War II. The Battle of Midway turned the tide of the war against the Japanese.

Chapter 4

1945

On August 6,1945 the United States dropped the first atomic bomb on Hiroshima. Japan surrendered on August 15,1945, officially ending World War II, but the war and destruction for the Japanese people did not end. On August 9, the Russians declared war against Japan, invading Manchuria, a region that is now the northeast corner of China bordering Russia. Setsuko and her husband lived in Manchuria at that time. The Japanese had occupied the region of Inner Manchuria since the Russio-Japanese War of 1904-1905. Now the Russians sought to reclaim this land.

At that time, the Japanese considered the Chinese low-class citizens and discriminated against them. The Chinese people were extremely poor, and most of the available employment was in labor jobs serving the Japanese people. There was also great animosity between the Japanese and Chinese, stemming from an event known as the Nanking Massacre— a six-week period in 1937 when the Japanese raped and killed an estimated 20,000 to 80,000 Chinese. Tensions already ran high in this region, even as Russia threatened to invade.

The Japanese army was spread out in the Pacific. Much of the land in China that was occupied by the Japanese was bordered by the Khingan Mountains, making an invasion difficult. The Japanese believed their territories were easy to defend and safe from attack—but they bet wrong. The Russians invaded directly through the mountains where Setsuko lived.

Suddenly, the Japanese were surrounded by enemies. They were murdered by the thousands.

Setsuko's husband was exempt from the army draft because he'd been born with a deformed arm, making it impossible to hold a rifle. The Russians captured him and sent him north to a concentration camp in Russia.

The Russians raped Japanese women by the thousands. However, they had a law forbidding the rape of a pregnant woman, since they wanted control over babies who would eventually populate their empire. At the time of her husband's capture, Setsuko was 22 years old and near the end of her pregnancy with her third child. A soldier attempted to rape her and was shot on sight by his own comrade for breaking Russian law. Setsuko was spared from rape, but the soldiers continued shooting. This time they wanted *her* dead. Setsuko felt the dirt hit her legs from the rain of bullets flying by her as she clutched her children and ran. She and her mother-in-law escaped to a refugee camp.

The camp was filled with women and young girls who had been raped by Russian soldiers. They sat in the dirt with expressionless faces. Flies swarmed around their female parts and open wounds—they had lost their minds. In the refugee camp on November 21, 1945, Setsuko gave birth to her third son.

Soon the Chinese found the refugee camp and destroyed it. Setsuko, her three sons, and her mother-in-law were on the run again. They stowed away on a gondola train along with many other Japanese people who were trying to hide. With her own eyes, Setsuko saw a Chinese man take a Japanese baby and throw him in the river to drown. She couldn't believe a human could be that cruel to an innocent child.

During the journey, her mother-in-law got sick and died. It was the Japanese custom to cremate the body after death and bury the ashes in the family cemetery. Despite hating this woman with all her being, Setsuko honored that tradition. She burned her mother-in-law's body but didn't have time to wait for it to burn completely. She poked the fire with a stick and gathered some of the small bones and fingers and put them in a handkerchief. Using strips of fabric, she tied her infant to her back along with the handkerchief and faithfully carried them both. Two years later, when she finally returned home, she would bury her mother-in-law's bones in Japan with her family to honor their custom.

Setsuko and her three sons hid from the enemy in a sugar cane field with a group of refugees. The children cried and gave away their hiding place. Mothers were pressured to kill their children for fear of being discovered. They took large leaves and covered their faces to suffocate them.

Setsuko was not able to bring herself to kill her children. She broke away from the group and traveled alone through the mountains and treacherous country. One day she heard a baby cry across the river. The cry tugged at her heart strings. She discovered its mother did not have enough milk to feed her baby. Despite being close to starvation herself, Setsuko miraculously had an abundance of milk in her breasts. She offered to feed the child in addition to her own infant.

The Chinese family was so grateful, they risked their own lives and hid Setsuko and her children. Setsuko stayed for almost eight months. One day the Russians came and raided the village looking for Japanese people. The Chinese family took Setsuko's children and spread them out to other families for safe keeping. They stuffed Setsuko in the stove to hide.

After the raid, some of the villagers got angry and called the Chinese family traitors for harboring Japanese people. It was no longer safe to stay there. But the Chinese family told friends in the next village to help Setsuko and her sons, and word quickly spread.

They created an underground railroad system to get Setsuko and her sons—ages five, two, and eight months—to the waterfront from the mountains. Through word of mouth, the Chinese told those who could be trusted to look for a Japanese woman and three small boys, hide them, and help them move from house to house in order to reach a boat bound for Japan.

With no map to guide them, Setsuko and her children travelled slowly from village to village, hiding in the mountains and the sugar cane fields along the way. One day she spotted some Russians down the road. Setsuko went into a farmer's shed and used a scythe to cut off her hair, disguising herself as a man.

They were starving. Desperate to survive, they ate what they thought was a dead dog in the road, but it wasn't a dog. It was a human body.

After two years, they finally reached Korea and made it on the very last boat travelling to Japan before the borders were closed. There were 2,000 people on that boat, and Setsuko had the only children on it. Everyone was shocked to see that they had survived when most refugees had been forced to sacrifice their children in their flight. People clamored to hold the children, but Setsuko grew tired of their questions and ignored them. She was anxious to get home and see her family. A journey that would normally take four days took Setsuko and her sons two years and eight months–mostly on foot.

An estimated 100,000 Japanese civilians died trying to return to Japan from Manchuria during the winter of 1945.

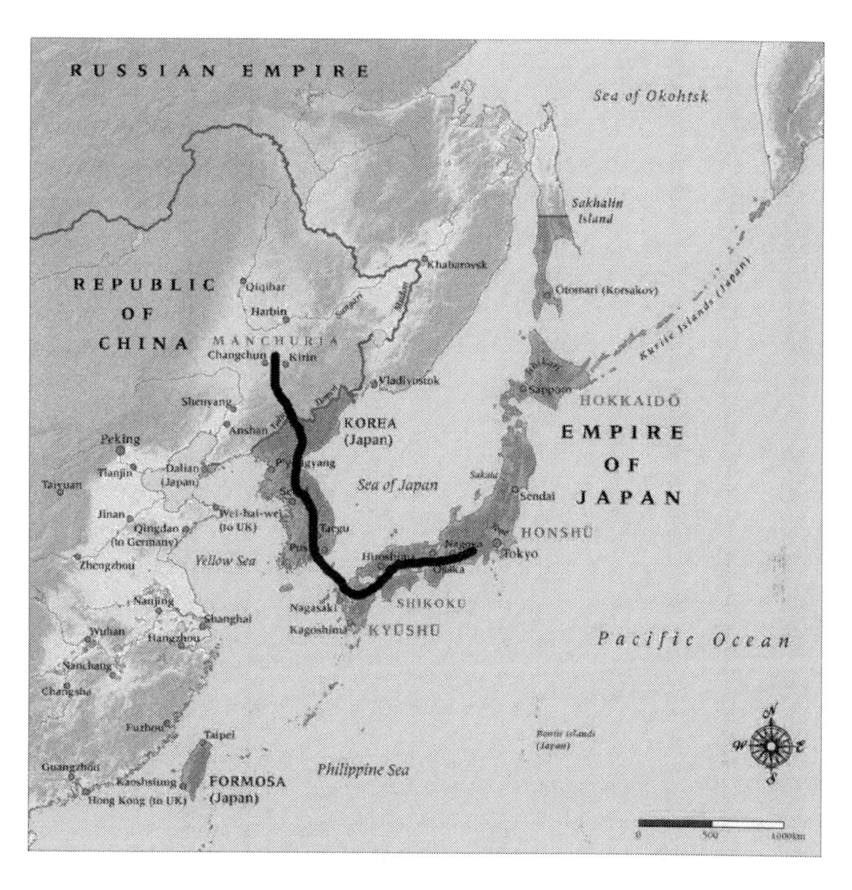

Setsuko's Journey
'Map of the Empire of Japan in 1914',
URL: https://nzhistory.govt.nz/media/photo/map-empire-japan-1914,
(Ministry for Culture and Heritage), updated 14-Aug-2014

Chapter 5

1948

In 1948, the boat finally arrived. Before anyone could leave the boat, Japanese officials required all the refugees to be stripped down naked and inspected for diseases, a process that took a couple of weeks. Syphilis was common because of the thousands who were raped, and any refugees who were deemed a risk to society were shipped to an island to die. Setsuko and her sons passed inspection and finally set foot on Japanese soil.

Setsuko swore she would never leave Japan again. By this time, she had been missing for nearly three years, and most of her family thought she was dead. While she was gone, her father had become quite the businessman. During the war, people traded their land and houses to him for a bag of rice. After the war, families started to return and wanted their homes back. Setsuko's father sold them back at a profit but reserved one house for Setsuko. He never lost faith that she would come back to him.

At 4:30 AM the same morning the boat docked, Setsuko's father awoke and told one of his four wives that Setsuko was home. She of course tried to convince him that Setsuko was dead, but Setsuko's father was certain that he "felt her soul return."

Although Setsuko was now back in her home country, it was the Japanese custom that the wife must return to her husband's family. She was not allowed to go back to her parent's house in Tokyo. Instead, she went to live with her husband's family in southern Japan and wrote a letter to her father telling him she had returned. Her husband had been missing for two years and eight months, but since there was no proof that he was dead, the only way she would be able to return to her parent's home was if she got a divorce. The Japanese custom only allowed this if the husband was missing for a minimum of three years. She stayed with her husband's family for the remaining months while her father arranged the paperwork for a divorce.

Those months were very difficult for Setsuko. Her husband's family was very wealthy and had lots of servants. They were embarrassed by Setsuko's ragged appearance and the callouses that she developed from living in the wilderness for so long. Even though she had risked her life to carry her mother-in-law's bones back to her homeland to be honored, her husband's family forced her to eat outside instead of at the table with the other women and children. Setsuko was bitter that they treated her so badly and couldn't wait to go home to her parents in Tokyo. Even the Chinese had been kinder to her than her own people.

After her divorce was settled, Setsuko was finally able to go home. She was so happy! However, her happiness was short-lived. Three days after the divorce was finalized, her husband returned. When he discovered she had divorced him, he was furious. He had been held in the Russian prison camp. Only fed once a day, tortured, and forced to work in extremely cold conditions, many of the prisoners died. He told Setsuko the only thing that kept him going was the hope that his wife and children were waiting at home for him. Feeling betrayed and angry, he took Setsuko's three sons away while she was at work one day. Although she had protected them through so many hardships, there was nothing she could do because Japanese women had no rights.

After her children were taken from her, Setsuko was distraught and depressed. She stayed in bed for three months. It angered her to see other young women laughing and having fun, dressed up in lipstick and high heels. Her pain was so deep, it seemed unfair that other people had happiness. She was lonely and felt that no one understood what she was going through.

Setsuko's father felt guilty for arranging the marriage and then the divorce that took the children away. He gave Setsuko the house he saved for her and told Setsuko he would pay for her to start a new life. He gave her money to go to typing school so she could work at the American Air Force Base. Setsuko always hated school. Now having freedom without any responsibilities, she set out to experience the youth that had been stolen from her. She was 23 years old and eager to start a new life. She went to parties and flirted with the American soldiers.

At times, the language barrier caused some amusing miscommunications. She and her sisters would walk by the soldiers as they would yell out "Hey there, cutie!" The Japanese girls took offense to this remark because in Japanese the word *cutie* means *cucumber.* The girls thought the soldiers were making fun of their figures, saying they were as straight as a cucumber with no curves.

Years went by and one day Setsuko got a phone call from the police station. They said they were holding a young boy claiming to be her son. When she arrived, she was reunited with her firstborn child. The younger two boys were not old enough to remember their birth mother, but Matsatoshe never forgot. He ran away from his father and stepmother to find her. He was ragged, barefoot, and dirty but Setsuko was overjoyed to see him. She took him home and cleaned him up. She bandaged his wounds where his stepmother had beaten him—she had tied him to a tree and whipped him with bamboo until his back was bare and bloody. Years later, while watching *The Passion of the Christ* in a movie theater, Setsuko sobbed at the scene where Jesus was whipped. The marks reminded her of those on her son's back. He was 12 years old.

Chapter 6

1957

After several months of goofing off, Setsuko eventually finished typing school and got a job at the Tachikawa Air Force Base. Setsuko's beauty attracted lots of young men. To show their affection, American servicemen would bring their special lady an orange. This was considered a rare treat because oranges were not native to Japan and came all the way from California. The other ladies in Setsuko's office would get jealous because her desk was often covered with oranges.

Setsuko in Tokyo

One of the men who courted her was named Clarence. He got into a fistfight with another soldier over her and broke his arm in the fight. He went to Setsuko's house and she took care of him. Clarence and Setsuko began dating, but her son was not happy about another man taking away his mother's attention. When Clarence came to visit, Matsatoshe would lie and say his mother was not home. Undeterred, Clarence was kind to Matsatoshe and took him to baseball games and movies. He eventually won him over, and for a while, the newly-formed family was happy.

Betty

On July 13, 1957, Setsuko casually strolled down the streets of downtown Tokyo. Clarence wanted her to live on the Tachikawa Air Force Base housing with him, but she insisted on living in the house that her father saved for her. It was sentimental. Walking had become more of a waddle recently, but she knew the exercise was good for her.

Suddenly, she felt a sharp pain and grabbed Clarence's arm. The baby was coming! Clarence and Setsuko's older brother quickly hailed a taxi. They each grabbed one of Setsuko's arms and helped her into the cab. Clarence started sweating profusely—he knew if the baby was born before they got to the American Air Force base, there would be a lot of red tape with the citizenship laws. He had orders to transfer back to the States soon, and he couldn't risk having to leave his new family behind!

Setsuko's contractions came faster. When they reached the gate, the military police stopped them. "This Japanese taxi does not have authorization to enter." They noticed the woman in labor and called for an ambulance. This was Setsuko's fourth baby and she knew there wasn't much time left. She argued with the guards as the ambulance arrived. "It coming! If I move legs, baby come out!" All the men panicked—none of them wanted to deliver a baby. A soldier waved them through, and the ambulance followed.

Setsuko's brother tried to help, but she swatted his hand away. She might be in labor, but she still had her modesty. Clarence yelled at the petrified taxi driver to go faster. He was covered in blood from holding Setsuko. When they arrived at the hospital, Clarence and Setsuko's brother helped her out of the car. A few minutes later, the baby was born just inside the front doors.

That baby was my mom.

Although not highly ranked, and with little income, Clarence somehow managed to raise $500 to cover the immigration costs to take his family and Matsatoshe overseas. By this time, Matsatoshe was 16 years old. Since he didn't speak any English, Setsuko translated for them during every meal. After Betty came along, he no longer got as much attention as he once did, and Matsatoshe decided that he didn't want to go to the States. With the painful memories of losing her son the first time, Setsuko began to doubt her own decision to leave.

Before entering the United States, it was mandatory to get a physical and cultural training in order to ease the transition of immigration. Setsuko went to the hospital for her physical and sat in the examination room holding four-month-old Betty, who was crying after receiving her shots. She decided to run away with her. She lied to the soldier who was standing guard that she needed to go outside and nurse the baby and would return soon. Holding Betty close to her, she took the train and ran away to her friend's house.

Once Clarence found out she was gone, he sent the military police and a Red Cross nurse after her. Knowing Setsuko had a friend, he went to her place to find her. Setsuko cried and told Clarence she didn't want to go to the States. He told her that she didn't have to go, but he was taking his daughter with him. The nurse was confused at the heart-wrenching situation, she didn't know what to do. Setsuko held her baby in her arms to feed her one last time. As she looked at the innocent baby's face, her heart broke. She decided this baby needed her more than her 16-year-old son did, so she decided to go to the States with Clarence.

Before Setsuko left for the States, she went to see her son one last time to try to convince him to go with her. She found Matsatoshe in the kitchen of the restaurant where he worked. He loved to cook and enjoyed having dinner ready for her when she got home from work every day. Having dinner with his mom was his favorite part of the day.

Setsuko held Betty in her arms and looked through the window of the restaurant at her son. He looked happy. She knew the move to a foreign country where he didn't speak the language would be very difficult for him. Her tears dripped on Betty's face. She decided it would be best for him to stay. She slowly walked away. Matsatoshe never knew his mother came to see him.

Setsuko was 31 years old and never saw any of her sons again.

Chapter 7

1958

A New Life Begins

In contrast to Setsuko, who was raised in the city of Tokyo, Clarence was from the country in western Maryland. He was raised Catholic, and his family did not approve of Setsuko being previously married. They liked it even less that she was Japanese–the enemy. They wouldn't let her come to church and excluded her from the family. With a brand-new baby to take care of, she was once again scorned for her ethnicity, living in a foreign country, and trying to learn a new language.

Japan did not have outhouses like Setsuko found in Maryland, and this was strange to her. She was also afraid of snakes, which were quite common there. Setsuko had never used a wood stove before and had no idea how to use the damper. She tried to start a fire, but instead filled the entire house with smoke.

The Maryland country was so remote, people used horses to travel between houses, and Setsuko grew extremely lonely. As soon as Clarence got back to the States, he took 30 days of leave and went straight to the woods. He loved to hunt and was gone for weeks at a time. When Clarence returned from his hunting trip, Setsuko demanded he send her to see her sister, Kimeko. Her sister had also married an American and was living in New York at the time.

Setsuko took the train to New York with difficulty, as she couldn't read any of the signs. When she was sitting in her seat, a man handed her a pillow. Bouncing a toddler on her lap was exhausting and she was so grateful for his kindness. He stood there with his hand stretched out, but she didn't understand what that meant. She had finally rocked Betty to sleep and laid her head on the pillow when the man rudely jerked the pillow out from underneath her. She didn't know the man had wanted a tip, an American custom.

Setsuko was thrilled to be reunited with her sister, but the happiness turned out to be short-lived. Her sister did not have any children and was particular about her house being clean. She was not happy about sticky toddler fingers marking her walls or dirty diapers being changed on her floor. Setsuko and her sister argued, and Setsuko called Clarence to come get her. Being lonely was better than this.

Three years after Betty was born, Setsuko gave birth to a boy, Eddie, who was born three months too early. He had to stay in the hospital for some time. Setsuko didn't have any friends where they were stationed, and Clarence was gone on active duty, so there was no one to watch Betty, who was prevented by hospital rules from visiting along with her mother. So Setsuko tied Betty's wrist to a tree in front of the hospital doors. When a woman from social services told her it was inappropriate, Setsuko argued with her and told the woman that *she* could watch Betty instead. The woman left her alone. Setsuko was out of options and stressed about her baby boy whose life hung in the balance. At that time, it was rare for babies born that early to live. Setsuko went to the hospital every day and manually expressed her milk for the hospital to use in their bottles. Eddie remained in the hospital for five months before he was healthy enough to come home.

Later, Donna Louise was also born prematurely at six months. She only lived for four days. Altogether, Setsuko had eleven pregnancies, six of which were born. The remaining five were miscarriages.

One day Setsuko received a letter from Japan. Her son Matsatoshe had joined a gang and gotten into a terrible knife fight. He was stabbed in the stomach and was in the hospital, unable to pay his bills. Barely surviving on what they had, Setsuko borrowed the money from her sister to pay the hospital bills. Matsatoshe recovered but was never able to have children as a result of the injury.

About that time, a man offered Setsuko a job sewing and mending clothes for the soldiers at the base. It paid five dollars a week. At that time, one month's electric bill was about three to four dollars, so Setsuko was thrilled to have the job. She was able to stay at home mending clothes while still taking care of her children. It took her three years, but she finally paid her sister back the money she borrowed for Matsatoshe's hospital bills. Setsuko worked in various places, including a sewing factory and as a maid in a hotel, until age 65.

Chapter 8

1975-1977

Setsuko raised two children, learned to drive, persevered through the language barriers and customs of a foreign country, and took the exams to become an American citizen. But her marriage to Clarence did not turn out to be a happy one. He walked out three times for several months at a time, leaving his family without enough money to pay bills. Once, the electricity was cut off.

Setsuko and Clarence separated when Betty was in high school. Betty stayed with Setsuko and Eddie went to live with Clarence. Setsuko made plans to move to Hawaii and live with her two sisters, Kimeko and Tomeko, after Betty graduated. Betty had already applied and was accepted into the University of Hawaii. She was a straight-A student, captain of the cheerleading team, and won many awards for her outstanding achievements. Clarence was old-fashioned and didn't believe that women needed to go to college, but Setsuko was adamant that her daughter get a higher education.

But Betty's high school sweetheart begged her not to leave the East Coast. They had met in the eighth grade and had been dating since the tenth grade. They continued to court even long distance when William (nicknamed Woody) transferred to a military academy. He proposed, and instead of moving to Hawaii with her mom, Betty got engaged to Woody at 19 years old. Setsuko was devastated once again to be saying goodbye to another child. Although it broke her heart, she knew she couldn't stand in the way of love.

But Setsuko found love again too. In Hawaii, she met a man and soon was engaged. But his daughters did not approve of her and made it clear how they felt. Setsuko did not want to come between them and broke off the engagement. She returned to the East Coast for Betty and Woody's wedding on July 30, 1977. Betty had just earned her associate degree and was 20 years old.

Not long after Setsuko's return to Maryland, Clarence slipped on some ice and broke his femur bone, which required a full body cast to repair. Although still angry with him for his desertion, Setsuko nursed him back to health. After a three-year separation, they decided to give the marriage another chance.

They went on to enjoy regular visits from their grandchildren, who have happy memories of spending time with them and fishing with Granddad. As a result of the accident, Clarence had a permanent limp for the rest of his life. Years later, when he had kidney failure, Setsuko took care of him every day around the clock until he died in 2001. To this day, she still wears the wedding ring he bought her.

Setsuko and Clarence

Chapter 10

1981

In contrast to Woody, who was six feet tall with a muscular frame, Betty was a petite four feet and ten inches and weighed 90 pounds soaking wet. Woody would often hoist Betty onto his shoulder and carry her one-armed across the hot sand at the beach. Despite her small physical stature, Betty inherited her mother's strength of character and perseverance. After a couple years in college, she and Woody decided to join the Army. In 1981, they became the first married couple to graduate Officer's Candidate School (OCS) in the same company, although in separate platoons.

After OCS, Betty went to Airborne School. She was often the first person to jump out of the plane but the last one to land on the ground. She was so light, the wind often blew her out of the drop zone and she had to run as fast as she could to meet up with her team.

The airborne class started out with about 20 women and 200 men, but the rest of the women either dropped out or failed because of the intense physical and mental challenges. Betty was the only female to graduate.

Chapter 11

1985

In 1985, Betty and Woody were captains in the Army. Betty was finishing her master's degree and was expecting her first baby. A few weeks before the expected delivery date, Setsuko went to visit them in Fort Hood, Texas to help with preparations. When Betty went into labor, there were complications–the baby was breech. Setsuko and Woody were there in the operating room when the baby finally arrived via emergency C-section. It was a girl, Jennifer Kimberly, named after Setusko's sister, Kimeko.

That baby was me.

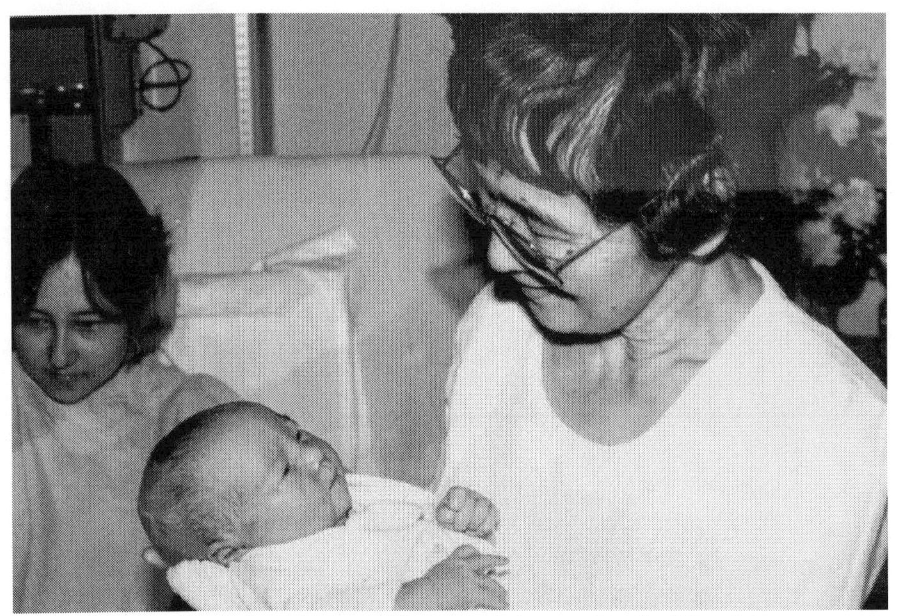

Betty, Setsuko, and Kimechan (picture taken by Woody)

Chapter 12

1988-1989

Three years later, Betty and Woody were stationed in Germany. Woody was a company commander and was in the field for weeks at a time. He carried on the military tradition from his father, who was also an Army ranger. His dad earned numerous medals in the Korean and Vietnam Wars and later in his career worked for the CIA. He is buried in Arlington National Cemetery.

In 1988, tensions were high. It was the fall of the Berlin Wall, which served as a physical symbol of the Iron Curtain during the Cold War. Military security was put on high alert. Betty was in the top percentage of the Army and had one of the highest military security clearances available. The Army offered her a position in the Special Operations division; however, Betty was pregnant with her second child at the time and was often called in to work at all hours of the night and day. She turned down the offer. She decided to retire from active duty and remain in the reserves. Daniel was born on April 23, 1988 in Heidelberg, Germany. A series of revolutions and political pressure led to the wall's final destruction on November 9, 1989.

After her children went to college, Betty got a position in Quantico, Virginia, working on military contracts until she retired in 2018 to take care of Setsuko full time.

Part 2

Kimechan

Without the "Hard" you would never even notice the "Happy,"
and that's the answer to the "Why."

–J. Kimberly Cartis

Chapter 1

1999

When I was 13, Mom was in a car accident that caused spinal injuries and sent her into a tailspin of health problems for several years. She got increasingly sick and fragile. We refer to this time period as "The Dark Years" because Mom doesn't remember two whole years. My brother Daniel was ten.

One day I was outside cutting the grass. The motor was loud, and I didn't hear Daniel calling my name. Finally, I looked up and saw him standing on the deck yelling for me with tears streaming down his face. I ran inside and found Mom unconscious on the floor. Mom has a petite frame, and she barely weighed 100 pounds, but Daniel's little ten-year-old body still couldn't lift her alone. We dragged her to the bedroom, lifted her into bed, and called Dad at work. Looking back now, I'm not sure why I didn't call an ambulance, except I think we had gotten used to Mom being sick and this wasn't the first time we found her on the floor. Another time she had passed out in our tiny half bathroom and I remember struggling against the door because her body was trapped behind it.

At some point, Mom decided she didn't want to be on medication anymore because the side effects were wrecking her body, but instead of getting better the withdrawal made her worse. By this time, I had given myself a crash course in taking care of the cooking, cleaning, laundry, and helping Daniel with his homework. We didn't have any family nearby and Dad was putting in long days at work. He was commuting an hour and a half one way to Washington, D.C. and double that on heavy traffic days. I remember bringing Mom a tray of Japanese food to her bed, because rice was the only thing she could keep down. We *always* used chopsticks when eating any Asian food, but Mom's hands shook so badly she couldn't even hold them. I went to the kitchen, got a spoon, and fed her myself.

Chapter 2

2000

One morning before the sun came up, Dad woke me and said he couldn't take any more days off work. He asked me to get in bed with Mom to keep her company. I remember climbing into the bed and looking at her. She was so frail. As the sun began to rise, my eyelids got heavy and I started to drift back to sleep. Mom called out my name and grabbed my hand. "Jennifer, don't go to sleep," she whispered desperately. "If you don't stay awake with me, I might not make it."

I'll never forget her fragile but urgent voice that day. Sometimes in those wee hours of the morning, when I know I need to get out of bed but want to succumb to the warmth of sleep, my mind returns to this moment and I struggle to fight it.

One day I noticed Mom's down comforter was getting ragged and torn. She was often cold and loved the warmth it gave her. I wanted to make her feel better, so my best friend Kristin and I decided to make her a new one. We weren't old enough to drive yet and had only used the sewing machine under supervision, but we were determined to try this project anyway. Mom was stuck in her room all the time and I wanted something to brighten her day.

I think it took us nearly three days. We ripped out the seams many times. The sewing machine kept getting jammed, and we made it way too big, but I remember how proud we were of that blanket cover. It made Mom smile. Kristin went on to get me through many dark times in the coming years.

The day I turned 15, Dad told me we were going to the DMV. I protested that I wasn't ready to take the driving test, but he insisted. He said that mom was too sick, and he didn't want her driving anymore. I had been studying the book to get my learner's permit for weeks, but I had terrible test anxiety. Missing six or more questions meant failure. I missed five. I drove us home that day.

Chapter 3

2001

On September 11, 2001, I was 16. Dad's mom called in a panic that morning and asked if Dad was okay. We hadn't heard from him since he left for work. We turned on the news and saw the devastating effects of the plane crashes that hit the Twin Towers and the Pentagon. My blood ran cold. Dad worked for the Metropolitan Police Department, a couple of miles from the Pentagon. We couldn't reach him on his cell phone because the signals were overloaded and jammed. So many people couldn't reach their loved ones.

Sometime later that day, Dad's call got through. He was okay, but he didn't come home until late that night. He had been in a meeting with the Chief of Police and other staff members when suddenly everyone's phones went off with news of what had happened. He stayed to help and bought food for the first responders.

I remember driving by the Pentagon days later and seeing the charred building. There was still smoke rising and ash floating in the air.

Chapter 4

2005

Mom eventually found new doctors. It took years, but with the help of new medical strategies and sheer determination, her health slowly improved. Mom and Dad were both in the Army reserves, but after 9/11 they were called on alert and told to be prepared for active duty. I had planned on joining the Army to pay for college and had already visited the recruiting office, but Daniel was still in high school at the time. Mom and Dad signed paperwork and gave me legal guardianship of him in the event of their death. I watched as he played paintball with his friends in the backyard one day and realized if something ever happened to our parents, he was going to need me around. The recruiting officer was disappointed, but I felt I had made the right decision. Dad deployed to Iraq when I was in college.

Daniel and I are the first to break military tradition in four or more generations, but Mom and Dad never pressured us to join. They wanted us to make our own life choices and I always appreciated that. I'm very proud of my military heritage. When I was in kindergarten, Dad returned from a seven-month deployment in the Persian Gulf War. He surprised me at a friend's house, and I'll never forget how happy I was to see him. Watching families reuniting with soldiers always brings tears to my eyes.

I went to college on school loans. Kristin was my roommate freshman year and we continued to live together on and off campus until we graduated.

Kimechan and Kristin in college

We formed other close friendships, and at the start of our junior year, we moved into a house with several other college girlfriends. We named our house the Greenhouse, a place for growth.

We took turns visiting each other's hometowns during school breaks. During one of the hometown visits we learned about a bombing in Iraq. Dad was deployed there at the time, and days before he had sent me pictures of the building where he worked—one of Saddam Hussein's old palaces. Watching the news, I saw the same building, now covered in rubble and smoke. I cried on Kristin's shoulder and felt sick.

I couldn't reach Dad. I sat on the couch all night flipping news channels, hoping to see something that could tell me if he was alive or not. Late the next night, while surrounded by my friends, Dad called me on my cell. I put him on speaker phone, because everyone wanted to hear what happened. He told us he had left the office early that day because he wasn't feeling well. Dad missing work for being sick was a rare occurrence. A couple of hours later, a missile went right through his office, killing 2 people and injuring 14.

Many years later, I found out that he helped sort through the wreckage and picked up the body parts of what was left of his friends and the soldiers he worked with. I will never know the extent of the tragedies he experienced that day.

Chapter 5

2006

I met a guy during a family vacation the summer between my junior and senior years and instantly fell head over heels. He lived several states away and we wrote a lot of letters. After just a few short months, he was already talking about proposing. Dad was still deployed, but he called me and gave his blessing if I decided that's what I wanted.

Right before Thanksgiving break, the Greenhouse Girls hosted "Friendsgiving," and I made the turkey. Just before we sat down to eat, I got *the* phone call. He broke up with me. Everyone was waiting for me to get off the phone so we could say grace and eat, but Kristin found me crying my eyes out in the darkness of the backyard. She went back inside and told everyone to start without me. She grabbed her car keys and a tissue box and drove me around in her car while I cried over my broken heart.

Eleven years later, over some shots of tequila, she told me that she stole his number out of my phone, found out he had been cheating on me, and reamed him out. Now that's a quality friend! However, I didn't know that in November 2006.

I told my mom that instead of doing Thanksgiving dinner with our family, I was going to drive the 12 hours to see him. Thinking back now, I want to roll my eyes at my naivete. I made up my mind that I was going, and nothing was going to stop me. Mom never lectured me. She never said, "That's the dumbest idea ever" or "Have some self-respect." She said, "Okay, I'll come with you." I left Grandmom and Daniel to eat Thanksgiving dinner by themselves. Love makes us do selfish things at times.

Three hours into our drive, right before we crossed the state line, we saw an accident off the highway. I didn't see any first responders, so I pulled over. There were several other cars pulled over too and I could see the drivers on their cell phones calling 911, but *no one* got out to help. At the time, I was on the volunteer rescue squad and a licensed EMT, so I got out and ran toward the wreck. There were wrapped presents strewn all over the highway and the car was flipped upside down. As I approached, I remembered my training–always ask how many people were in the vehicle. I could see an empty car seat and my heart was in my throat. A woman crawling out of the wreck told me there were three people in the car, but I only counted two. I searched the ground, tearing through the piles of Fall leaves. Then I saw him, face down in the mud, he had been thrown at least 20 feet from the car. I tried to get a bystander to help me, but he insisted that we not touch him and that we should wait for the ambulance. I argued that he would die if we didn't help him. He finally agreed to help me. I showed him how to turn the victim so we could keep his spine intact as much as possible. Then he disappeared, leaving me alone with the injured man. Both of his legs were broken, his face was smashed, his teeth were broken and loose, and his mouth was full of debris. I cleared his airway the best I could. He was unconscious, but I spoke softly to him and tried to comfort him.

It felt like forever, but the ambulance, police, and fire trucks finally arrived. While everyone was preoccupied with the other injuries, I grabbed a first aid kit and bandaged the woman's hand. She explained that they were going to visit their grandkids for Thanksgiving and lost control of the car. She thanked me for helping her and asked for my address. As I wrote it down, I noticed I was shaking from the adrenaline and struggled to form the letters. We said goodbye. Then Mom and I got back in the car and finished the trip.

Much to my disappointment, I couldn't change my boyfriend's mind about breaking up with me. Mom held my hand while I cried all the way home, but even though my heart was broken, I felt like the trip was not in vain. Although I had felt powerless and hurt, I had been able to help someone who was hurting more than I was.

After that heartbreak, the demands of senior year, pulling overnight shifts at the rescue squad, working a part-time internship at the county, dealing with the worry of Dad being deployed in a war zone, and being away from Grandmom and Mom, the stress really started to get to me. Inside, I was slowly declining. I was depressed and lonely, despite having tons of friends. My wrists physically ached and I considered cutting myself. It felt like it wasn't fair that the outside of my body looked fine when the pain I was feeling was so deep, so invisible to everyone else. I wasn't looking for attention–I just wanted the inside of me to match the outside. I thought about it for several weeks, maybe months.

One day on a rescue squad shift, we answered an attempted suicide call. I remember sitting with the patient in the back of the ambulance during transport and looking into her eyes. They looked dead inside, like she had completely lost all hope. I looked at her bandaged wrists. I thought about Grandmom and all the horrible things she endured. I thought about Mom and all the struggles she went through in the Army. I thought about how my problems didn't even come close to theirs. I felt guilty. I couldn't let them down by giving up. I decided in that ambulance that I would never again consider cutting my wrists.

But Grandmom did cut her wrists. I didn't find this out until 13 years later. I was shocked when I found out that Grandmom attempted suicide, but it's a very important layer of her extraordinary story. She didn't try to kill herself when she was married at 17 to a terrible man in China, not during the war, not as a refugee forced to eat a dead soldier to stay alive, not when her three boys were stolen from her, not when her baby girl died four days after birth, not when her fourth son Eddie committed suicide after a life of drugs, not when her American neighbors trampled her laundry and called her a "dirty Jap," not when her second husband left her and she had to fend for herself in a country where she didn't speak the language. She slit her wrists and tried to die... after her last remaining child grew up and left home. She thought she no longer had a purpose and that she didn't matter anymore. In the hospital, Mom begged her to live. I was born a couple years later. If she hadn't chosen to live that day, I would never have had the gift of experiencing her love. Grandmom is my hero, not because she is extraordinarily strong, but because in her weakest, darkest moments, she chose not to give up.

Later that semester, I received a package at the Greenhouse–a fruit basket. It was from the family in the car accident. The card said, "Thank you for saving my life that day." The man had lived.

Even though I was finding strength and purpose, I was still struggling with how to deal with the stress. One night during one of my rescue squad shifts, I was driving a patient to the hospital. I got disoriented in the dark and finally had to call headquarters and get directions. When we got to the hospital, I was so rattled I couldn't get the ambulance backed in the correct way. The chief lost his patience with me and took over. I was humiliated. I could feel myself falling apart. That same week, I turned in my resignation. I couldn't risk someone getting hurt because I had trouble focusing. I cried when my team said they would miss me.

That same year, I ran a half marathon. At the end of the race, I was so exhausted I could barely put one foot in front of the other. Mom broke from the crowd, held my hand, and ran the last mile with me. We crossed the finish line together. The truest example of beauty, femininity, and strength, she has taught me so many things.

Daniel and I have always been there for each other when things got hard. One of my happiest memories was when he told me he was enrolling at the same college. We look a lot alike–so much that people frequently asked if we were twins. I used to tell them we were and joked that I was the smart one and that's why I was three grades ahead. The joke is funny because *he's* the smart one. A computer genius. A natural born athlete. I've always been super proud of him, not just because he's so talented, but because he is one of the best humans I've ever met.

When Daniel and I went home at the end of the semester, we spent Christmas with Mom and Grandmom. Dad was still in Iraq at the time. Daniel had wanted a guitar to play to impress a girl. Mom said he could pick one out for his Christmas present, so we went to the store to get it. On the way, we stopped at the pet store, just for fun. The salesclerk asked if I wanted to hold a puppy. It was love at first sight. I felt her soft fur, held her, and I couldn't let go. Mom and Daniel watched us. I didn't know it at the time, but they had been worried about me. That's the thing about being sad–you can't see outside your pain and realize how much the people around you love you. Daniel told Mom to use the money for his guitar and buy the puppy for me instead. When we got home, Grandmom asked where the guitar was. Daniel pointed to the wiggly puppy. "Here's my guitar, Grandmom." We all laughed together, and it felt so good.

He eventually got the guitar. And the girl. He married his high school sweetheart. To this day, she's one of my best friends.

Daniel and Kimechan

Grandmom knew I was sad about my heartbreak. One day she told me, "Kimechan, I had hard life. Lots of struggle. This not so bad. You will heal." I knew she was right.

Almost ten years later she apologized to me. Her eyes were full of remorse. "Kimechan, I know I tell you don't be sad about that boy. Your life not so hard. I sorry. I should never tell you. It's not your fault Grandmom have hard life. I love you." I reassured her that it was okay, I needed to hear it. Then she hugged me and said with a smile, "Lots of bad things happen. But ok now. I have you. You make me happy."

Chapter 6

2007

I graduated college with a degree in International Business. Grandmom always told me, "Study hard, Kimechan. Someone can steal everything you have, but they can never steal your mind." She barely has an eighth-grade education and told me she was a holy terror in school. She stole other kids' lunch boxes, tied girls' braids to their desks, and climbed out the classroom window to play hooky as often as possible. Truly a wild child who hated school, she still loves to read. She made me promise to go to college. She keeps my graduation picture near her bed so she can look at it every day.

Slowly, things started to get better. Kristin and I started a penny jar during our freshman year and had been planning a cross-country road trip after graduation. We were so excited about it and planned to leave the next Friday as soon as I got off work. I had an internship my senior year working as the tourism coordinator with the county. There was a guy there who had asked me out earlier that year. We went on a lunch date, but before we made it back to his truck, I told him bluntly that I wasn't interested in a relationship. He was almost nine years older than me and had a full-time job. I just wasn't interested at the time and was consumed with college life. Nevertheless, he continued to be polite to me throughout the year and I noticed he was always a nice guy to everyone in the office.

I guess I was feeling optimistic and excited about the upcoming trip, because the day we were leaving I asked on a whim if he would kiss me.

He obliged. One simple kiss. When our lips touched, it was complete magic—it felt like fireworks. I was not expecting *that.*

We said goodbye and I went back to the Greenhouse to help pack the car. Kristin wanted to know why my hands were shaking but I didn't have the courage to tell her that I had just kissed a guy that I had no interest in dating. After all, I hadn't shown great judgement in the last one. It didn't go well when I finally told her later that summer and she learned I kept it from her.

The road trip was amazing. After our 14-day adventure I went back to work to complete my internship. It was a little awkward seeing Kevin again after our kiss. I put in my two weeks' notice and let him know that I had taken a job in Washington, D.C. He asked if he could take me out for a "bon voyage" dinner. I said yes, and the rest is history. In 2019 we celebrated ten years of marriage together.

Chapter 7

2008

After college, I worked for a year in Washington, D.C. I was a project manager responsible for getting office furniture delivered inside the Pentagon and worked long hours. Whenever a new general or admiral rotated in, they would often change the furniture or redecorate for them. Many of my projects were for offices located in the "E ring," which is the outer hallway with all the VIPs. One of those projects was to get a custom bookcase made for the Chief of Naval Operations, the highest-ranking officer in the United States Navy. I had to wait for him to leave his office before I could go inside and take measurements of the room. I was nervous when I talked to him while I waited. He had a lot of bodyguards.

The firing rate among new project managers was high. One had to prove they could handle high pressure situations before making it past the 90-day review process. One of those tests was to deliver important documents in downtown D.C. traffic while driving the boss's brand-new Porsche and parallel parking on a busy street. This time, I nailed it.

I brought Mom to work with me one day and gave her a tour of the Pentagon. It felt special walking the halls with her and listening to her reminisce about her Army days. She talked about how hard it was having to be on call 24/7, reporting for duty at all hours when she had two young kids at home—finding a babysitter in the middle of the night was nearly impossible. When I was a baby, I often spit up all over the back of her uniform as she was walking out the door. Mom's stories always encouraged me when I felt overwhelmed with the stresses of working on high-profile projects.

During my lunch breaks, I often visited the memorial chapel that was built to commemorate 9/11. I sat there and thought about all the people that lost their lives in the exact location I was standing. One day they announced there would be a parade inside the Pentagon at noon. My experience with veterans and parades thus far had been Fourth of July celebrations and an old man in a uniform sitting in the back of a vintage car. We would smile and wave at him from the curb while someone threw candy. This was not that kind of parade. There was no confetti or balloons. I stood there, waiting, wondering why no one was smiling. Then I saw them. Not old men from a long-ago war. These were soldiers who were kids just like me, some of them even younger. They barely looked 18 and had *fresh* wounds. Some were on crutches with missing limbs, one had a burn that covered the entire side of his face, one had a missing eye. Another rolled right by me in a wheelchair. I was close enough to look into his eyes. They were distant and unfocused. I knew there was a war going on in Iraq. My own father was deployed there for 15 months. But until that day, I didn't understand what that truly meant. All I could do was stand there and cry.

Chapter 8

2009

Kevin and I dated long distance for a year while I was in Washington, D.C. We got married September 5, 2009. People thought I was crazy for leaving such a prestigious job, but I absolutely loved the small-town life with Kevin. We knew we wanted to start a family soon, so we opted for a simple wedding to save money. Daniel made my wedding cake and paper cranes for the tables in honor of our Japanese roots. Grandmom taught him origami when we were kids. I never could get the hang of it.

Kristin and I spent hours as little girls planning our weddings. We would often curl up on the couch in our college dorm room, flip through wedding dress magazines and procrastinate on exams. One time I joked that if she ever made me mad, I would pick the ugliest shade of yellow for her maid of honor dress. After college Kristin followed through with her dream to live out West. I reneged on our plan and stayed behind for a boyfriend and felt guilty as hell. The long distance was hard on the friendship. We always had a sort of weird telepathy thing going on and always seemed to know what the other person was thinking despite having very different personalities, but there was no denying that we had drifted apart for the first time in our friendship. I knew I broke her heart by not going with her and I wasn't sure she would come to the wedding. But she showed up, because that's what best friends do. And she wore a yellow dress.

I always prayed that God would allow Grandmom to live long enough to see me on my wedding day. Grandmom, Mom, Kristin, and the

Greenhouse Girls helped me get ready and lace up my wedding dress. It was one of the most special moments in my life.

Chapter 9

2010

Finding out I was pregnant was one of the most exciting moments of my life. I had always wanted to be a mom. Even as a little girl, I was always playing house with my dolls. Grandmom's and Mom's stories inspired me, and I loved hearing all of them. The irony is, Grandmom never aspired to be a mom, but didn't have a choice in the days of arranged marriages. Mom wasn't ready to become a mother either. She was at the height of her career as a captain in the Army and her position as branch chief had already been publicly announced. Life proved it had other plans when I came along. When her commanding officer found out that she was pregnant, he became furious, withdrew the position, and gave it to a male officer. Instead of dwelling on her disappointment, Mom decided to pursue her master's degree.

My excitement over my own pregnancy was short-lived. At ten weeks, I started bleeding and Kevin rushed me to the ER. We waited all night for results while my bleeding continued to get worse. When the doctor told me they couldn't find a heartbeat, I vomited in the trash can beside me.

I was one of the first among my friends to get pregnant and didn't know anyone who had experienced a miscarriage. I had no idea what to expect. After several days of the most intense pain and cramping imaginable, I felt my uterus contract when I was in the shower. With a sharp pain, the gestational sac came out. I'll never forget how devastated I felt when I saw the drain catch it—the water swirling around the tiny sac. Kevin held me while I cried. It was August first. Kevin's birthday.

But the heartache was far from over. The doctors discovered large cysts that engulfed both of my ovaries. They feared if they were left any longer, they would start to twist and rupture, eliminating all chances of ever conceiving a baby. Because of the high risk, they didn't want to do a laparoscopic surgery and instead wanted to open me up completely. I was sent to a specialist and had surgery two weeks after the miscarriage. We discussed all the risks and considered freezing my eggs, but the procedure would have taken more time and my doctor advised against any delays. I'll never forget waking up in the recovery room, completely panicked, with only one question. *Could I still have a baby*? The nurse patted my arm and gave me the news. The answer was *yes*. If it wasn't for that miscarriage, they would have never discovered the cysts in time before they ruptured. That baby I lost probably saved my life.

Kevin stayed by my side and supported me through it all. He crawled into the hospital bed with me and held me close. I knew no matter what happened we would be okay.

Chapter 10

2011

Four months later, I got pregnant again. The pregnancy was difficult due to my recent major surgery and I was also diagnosed with preeclampsia. I was induced at 38 weeks. After 17 hours of labor "Little Kimmy" was born, a healthy baby girl, eight pounds nine ounces. The spitting image of me.

FOUR GENERATIONS

Chapter 11

2012

Eight months later I was pregnant again. One of the Greenhouse Girls came to visit me. She was pregnant with her first baby and we couldn't wait to celebrate together. The morning she was scheduled to visit, I started bleeding. I'll never forget opening the front door and bursting into tears as she hugged me. She drove me to the doctor's office and held my daughter during my ultrasound while Kevin rushed from work to the doctor's office. This time when I looked at the screen, I knew. No heartbeat.

Grandmom squeezed me in a tight hug on my next visit. She had experienced five miscarriages of her own. She understood my pain. "Kimechan, you are pin in Japanese fan. Without mama everything fall apart. Your family need you. You be okay." Her compassion always comforted me.

Chapter 12

2013

A few months later, I was pregnant again. This pregnancy was also high-risk. At 38 weeks I started having contractions and went to the hospital. They told me it was false labor, but they would monitor me overnight.

We went home just after midnight. When I got up later that morning, I was in so much pain I had to hold onto the walls and lean on Kevin while he guided me down the hallway. He wanted to take me back to the hospital, but I refused. I couldn't take another false labor report.

It just so happened that I had a checkup already scheduled at nine that morning. It's a good thing that we went, because they immediately sent us to the hospital. "Little Daniel" was born via emergency C-section that day, nine pounds seven ounces. The spitting image of my brother.

After my second baby was born, I knew I needed to make some lifestyle changes. I was unhealthy and overweight and didn't have the energy to keep up with two toddlers. Grandmom inspired me to get back into exercising.

Grandmom loves to exercise. Before she gets out of bed each morning, she does 100 leg lifts in each direction and moves her arms from side to side. We always joked about not wanting to sleep with Grandmom when we were kids because you were sure to get kicked in the head or smacked in the face during her morning calisthenics. Grandmom was a fitness instructor at the senior citizen community center for two years in her seventies. She took me one time when I was 15 and literally danced circles around me. One of the old people asked why I was sitting down during one of the songs. I said because I was tired, and they all had a good laugh. That story still comes up every Christmas, much to my chagrin.

Finally motivated to embark on my own fitness journey, I discovered a love for Crossfit training and how lifting weights made me feel strong. Every year there is a competition called the Open where you can test your progress. One time, Grandmom and my parents came to watch me. The workout required a chest to bar pullup, which is just what it sounds like. Much to my disappointment, I couldn't do any, but there was a modification or "scaled" version available. I was faced with choosing the safe option, something I knew I could do, or going for the more advanced move and risk failing in front of my family. I decided to go for it. I did 24 chest to bar pullups that day. I'll never forget how proud I was, going straight for Grandmom's hug after I was done.

Chapter 13

2015

Less than a year after my son was born, I got pregnant again. It was my fifth pregnancy in five consecutive years. Since I had a pattern of miscarriages before a birth, Kevin and I were cautiously optimistic. We didn't want to get our hopes up only to be devastated again.

Despite our concerns, my pregnancy progressed, and we were both healthy. Mom and Dad lived more than two hours away. I was worried Kevin wouldn't make it to the hospital in time from his office, which was at least an hour and a half away. Thirty minutes after he got home one evening, my water broke. The doctor let me pull the baby out myself. It was an incredible experience. "Baby Belle" is named in honor of Kristin who loves books–Belle is her favorite Disney princess. She was eight pounds, ten ounces, Grandmom's first blue-eyed baby.

Three kids. Ages three and under.

Grandmom with her three great-grandkids

Motherhood

Grandmom shared her extra milk each time she had a baby. Mothers in Japan (and later in the United States) would bring her their babies when they didn't have enough. I never read a single book on breastfeeding when I was pregnant. After my oldest was born, I quickly discovered my error. I had no idea how hard it would be.

My daughter got teeth at four months old and soon started using those razorblades to draw blood. I was in tears. I called Grandmom, crying. She said, "Pinch baby nose, close one second. She will open mouth to breathe. She let go." I tried it. Sure enough, it worked. I was so grateful for her advice.

Grandmom inspired me to help others whenever I could. I often had an oversupply of milk like Grandmom and donated to several moms. One baby I donated for was a foster baby.

During one of our visits with Grandmom, I discovered lice on *all three* kids. I panicked. Grandmom came into the bathroom where I was doing their hair treatments and saw the stress on my face. "Kimechan, when I was in China, all the time I have bugs in my hair. Now you have medicine for this. You be okay." She was right. It was just a bug.

But here's an ugly truth about me: Grandmom's heroic life did not always inspire me. There was a time when it did the opposite. She managed to keep three young kids alive during a war, and I was struggling to keep three young kids (or even just one!) alive until my husband came home from work. She washed her clothes on river rocks, and I cried because I couldn't keep up with the laundry in my washing machine. Comparing myself to her situation just sank me deeper and deeper into a cycle of guilt and depression, overwhelmed with the pressures of motherhood.

One day Grandmom told me it wasn't my fault her life was so hard, being a mom *is* really hard. On another occasion, I remember sobbing on the phone with my mom and telling her that I didn't know how she raised me and my brother. She didn't give me a speech about how easy I had it these days. Instead, she told me that nothing she ever did in the Army was as hard as motherhood. She's a lieutenant colonel. She jumped out of planes and was pushed to physical breaking points, yet none of those hardships even came close to the challenges she faced as a parent. It took me awhile, but I finally realized that I was becoming my worst enemy in my own mind. This recognition broke a very negative cycle in my perception, and I came to this conclusion: There will always be someone who has it worse than you–let that give you perspective, but don't let it give you permission to feel unworthy.

In January 2019, I was invited to be a guest speaker at a mom's group. I shared about my struggles in early motherhood and how Grandmom and Mom helped me get through it. Now, when I carry my babies, I think about Grandmom carrying hers through the mountains of China and it inspires me to be the best mother and person that I can possibly be.

Chapter 14

2017

Grandmom has a special gift. She can predict a baby's gender before it's born. She was so accurate, that in the days before ultrasounds, people would come to her village in Japan to see her so they could get a prediction, hoping for boys to carry on the family name. She says that she can tell by how soft or sharp the lines and features are in the mother's face but says it's easier to tell if she knows the mother before she is pregnant. Grandmom accurately predicted the genders for all my babies, as well as for my mom's pregnancies for me and my brother. I do not have this gift. I am wrong every time.

A friend of mine wanted Grandmom to do a gender prediction for her. Grandmom guessed a girl, but I was skeptical about this prediction. After all, she didn't know my friend before she was pregnant and there was the fact that Grandmom was 95 years old. I was worried about her losing her 100% accuracy streak. Miss Leona was born the next May.

Chapter 15

2019

True to their Japanese heritage, Grandmom and Mom are very tidy. I remember Grandmom's scissors were neatly kept in the exact same drawer my entire childhood. Mom taught me to write in a steno pad and journal to keep life activities organized, long before the days of technology and smart phones. Growing up with their organized habits inspired me to look for ways to be more efficient, but after having three kids close together, life got chaotic. I found myself struggling to keep up. Nevertheless, I kept experimenting with new routines and systems to help streamline the work and I shared those ideas with friends. I found peace in pursuing a Minimalist lifestyle to help with keeping things in order. In February of 2019, I started my own business in professional home organizing.

The Storm

Not all storms come to disrupt your life, some come to clear your path.

—Author Unknown

On June 7, 2019, my husband went in for a routine gallbladder surgery. It was a quick 45-minute procedure and he was expected to go home that same afternoon. It didn't go as planned. The surgeon called me three hours into surgery and said there were complications and he had no idea how much longer it would be. I sent a text to Kristin with the update and she immediately called me. I was crying too hard to form any words, but I didn't need to say anything. At this point we had been friends for 22 years.

I'll never forget how scared I was in that waiting room. The doctor finally came out five hours later. He said the entire area was diseased and abnormally shaped, something he might expect in someone who was 70, not someone young and healthy. He had never seen anything like it on any of his previous cases. It took an hour on the operating table just to figure out a plan of what to do. The gallbladder was fused together in layers of fat and blood vessels, encased like a bird's nest. He explained that instead of pulling it out smoothly, they had to carefully cut layer by layer for several hours, cauterizing after every slice, causing a lot more trauma than expected, and it was very dangerous. It ruptured and leaked in several places.

I stood there with tears streaming down my face. I was in shock that we had no idea it was that far damaged. I kept thinking to myself, as long as I can see him, everything will be okay. Then I saw him. Everything was *not* okay. He looked like death. He woke up confused. I held his hand and did my best to explain what happened without scaring him, but I had to quickly walk outside to vomit. Just then my friend, who was an ICU nurse, called to check on me. I answered the phone and started hyperventilating. She told me to breathe. Panic attacks are a funny thing, you forget how to do something so basic. I'll never forget her reaching out to me in such a dark moment as I stood outside in the pouring rain, struggling to regain control.

The doctor wanted to monitor Kevin leave him. A friend brought me an overnight bag to the hospital. She included a brand-new soft blanket which I was so grateful to have in that cold room.

The next night Kevin developed a fever. I knew something was very wrong. It was so high the nurses refused to tell me the actual number. They started covering his body with ice packs and called the doctor. I started sobbing. One of the nurses grabbed my shoulders and hugged me. I could see the worry in her eyes. Kevin was completely pale and sweating, and his body wouldn't stop shaking. I've never been more scared in all my life. I climbed into the hospital bed next to him, trying to be careful not to hurt him. My husband has a very dry sense of humor that always made me laugh when we were dating (and made me roll my eyes sometimes in marriage). This would have been the moment he would have joked about it being payback for when *he* was the one getting in the hospital bed to comfort *me*. He didn't crack a single joke.

I couldn't sleep. My mind drifted back to that early morning when Mom was so sick and begged me to stay awake with her. I could still hear her voice. "*Wake up, Jennifer. If you go to sleep, I might not make it.*" I was wide awake. Kevin dozed on and off. I was never so happy to hear him snore. At least then I could close my eyes and listen to him breathing.

By morning they were able to get his temperature under control, but even under a constant flow of antibiotics and medication, he was still fighting a low-grade fever. I ordered him breakfast and tried to convince him to eat, but his hands were shaking so badly from the pain, he couldn't lean forward in the bed to eat. I opened the Italian ice and spoon fed it to him. This wasn't my first rodeo in taking care of someone.

On the third day, the doctor was concerned that he might need another surgery and ordered a CAT scan and more tests. They wouldn't let me go with Kevin for the CAT scan, so I paced the room like a caged tiger. After he got back, I helped him from the bathroom. Then he turned and faced me. His face turned white and suddenly he collapsed. I caught him under his armpits right before his head hit the bathroom door.

They told me that I couldn't lay down next to him anymore because the risk of infection was too high. My heart broke. I just wanted to listen to his heartbeat. It's always been my favorite way to fall asleep. It reminded me of a teddy bear my parents got for me when I was four years old. When you squeezed it, his heart would make a "thump" sound. I still have it.

The report from the CAT scan showed severe inflammation but no infection. We were so relieved that they wouldn't have to operate again, but his oxygen had dropped. The chest x-ray showed his lung was partially collapsed. We had tried to give him a shower but as soon as the water hit his body, he started to shake violently and we had to rush him to the bed, soap and all.

After five days in the hospital the fever finally broke. We were relieved to finally be able to go home. When we left the hospital, no one had any idea how long his recovery would be—after all, no one expected him to be in the hospital for five days for a simple outpatient procedure. Thankfully, after the fever was gone and with the use of a breathing machine to expand his lungs, his body was able to start healing.

The following weeks proved challenging. I was juggling the needs of Kevin's recovery and the litany of demands that three small humans require. I had gone five days without sleeping, except for a few 15-minute increments. My hair fell out in handfuls from the stress. Kevin had to sleep in the recliner because it was too hard for him to get in and out of our bed. It was almost a month before he recovered enough to sleep next to me. I will never take that for granted again.

But I didn't get through that experience alone. Our community reached out and supported us. Various family members kept the kids while we were in the hospital, and friends brought us meals. Kristin and her husband sent care packages and a playlist with songs about overcoming adversity. Mom came to help. I was *so* happy to see her. There's nothing like a hug from your mother when you're under immense stress. After a couple of weeks, Daniel and his wife came to visit and took the kids fishing so Kevin and I could go out on a lunch date. They were the best tacos I had ever eaten.

We had made it through the storm, together.

Photo by Julie

Later that summer, I went to visit Grandmom. She wrapped me in her arms and held me tight. She poured me some tea, and we sat at the kitchen table.

Epilogue

I hope this story inspires you *never to give up,* the way Grandmom and Mom have inspired me, and serves as a reminder not to live as a victim of your circumstances forever. Stand up for yourself. And above all, choose love instead of hate.

A wealthy man once asked Grandmom for the chance to do a documentary on her life. She declined, feeling it unnecessary. She only granted me permission to share her story because she saw how much it meant to me. The weight of that responsibility was paralyzing to me for a long time.

For years I stuffed notes in a drawer and told myself I would get to it *one day,* but the task felt too daunting. I had convinced myself that this wasn't anything like my previous aspirations. I wanted to record a century of important history intertwined throughout four generations. I'm far from being a historian and I had never written a book. It felt impossible. When I mentioned to my sister-in-law, Meghan, about my dream to one day write a book, I said it was a lofty goal and I didn't have any idea how I would accomplish it. I'll never forget what she said to me. "Jen, I've never seen you *not* follow through with something you set out to do. As far as I'm concerned, the book is already done." Her words kept replaying in my head.

After my husband's surgery scare, I decided I wasn't going to wait any longer. I realized the cliché is too true–we are not guaranteed tomorrow. I decided just to start typing. And here we are at the end of *the* book. With the encouragement of friends and Meghan's unwavering faith in me, I finished that lofty goal. Here's the life lesson: sometimes the good choices are hard. And uncomfortable. Do it anyway.

Now I intend to share Grandmom's extraordinary life with the world until the day I die, to inspire as many people as possible.

People will claim there is no way all these things really happened. I can assure you that calling this fiction would compliment my writing far more than I deserve. I'm not skilled enough to imagine this many complicated layers of story lines. Others will no doubt say that parts were embellished for dramatic effect. To that I say, this book was not written for entertainment. This is for my children, and it's bigger than just "a good read" to our family.

This is our legacy. This is *a story worth telling.*

Photos

Kimechan with Little Kimmy, Little Daniel, and Baby Belle

Recreating the look, Christmas 2018
Having fun playing dress up with Grandmom and Meghan (bottom right corner)

The Shibuya sisters
Setsuko, Kimeko, and Tomeko

Dad, Mom, and Kimechan

Grandmom and Kimechan, age 2

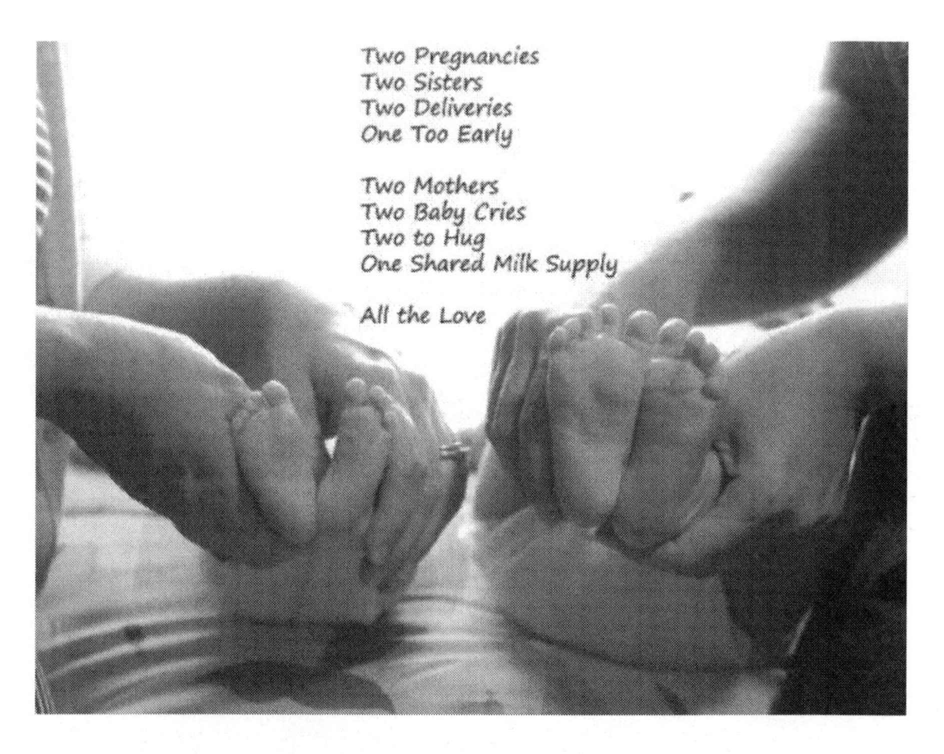

Sharing the love

My friend, who got the gender prediction from Grandmom, shared her breast milk with her nephew. He was born too early due to complications. She and her sister had their babies two weeks apart. I had the privilege of taking their newborn pictures and wrote this poem for them.

Grandmom and Kristin, August 2019

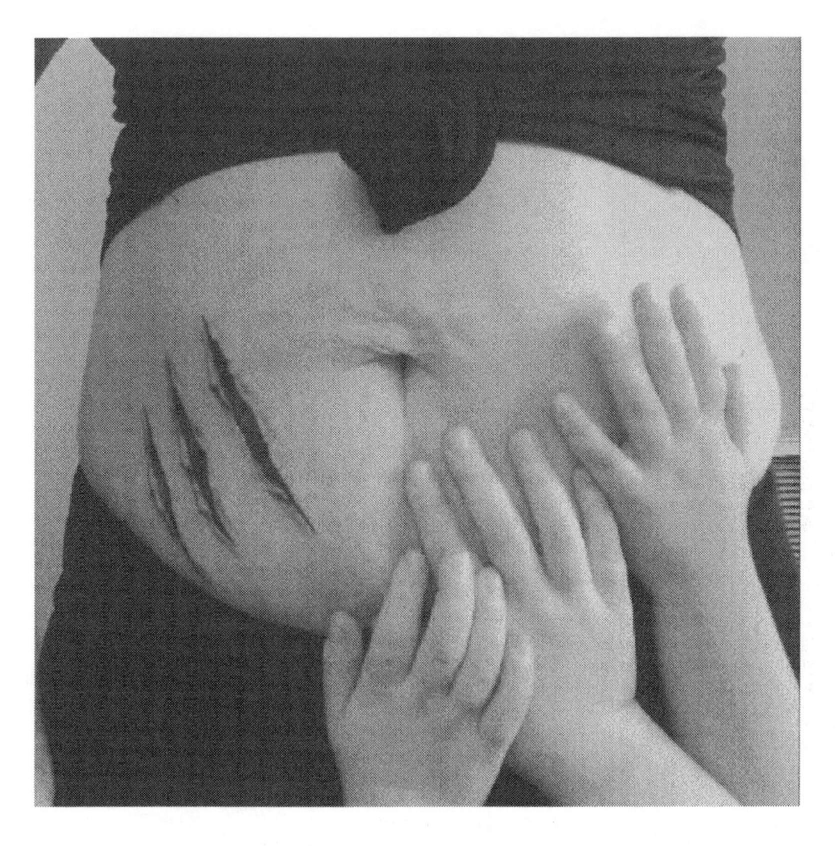

Earning my stripes

I got a tattoo to celebrate my mommy tiger stripes and scars. It represents the devastating feeling I had when the doctor told me that I might never have a baby, for the babies I carried who clawed their way out, for the ones I never got to hold, for the moments I had to claw my way out of dark holes and rise, and finally for being able to embrace my imperfections and learn to love myself.

Three generations
(Left to right) Kimcchan, Setsuko, and Betty

Grandmom, 96 years young

To hear Grandmom tell her story in her own words and to see additional pictures, please follow our Facebook page *A Story Worth Telling*.

If this book touched your heart, or you have an inspiring story about overcoming adversity please send us a message, Grandmom and I would love to hear it!

Acknowledgements

To my family, thank you for always being my biggest supporters. To my husband, who chooses to love me through all my imperfections–I love you. To Kristin, for being my best friend through the fun times as well as the dark ones, and for the many hours you put into helping me get this book published (and for being willing to help even before you knew you were in it). To the Greenhouse Girls and all the memories we share together. To Sharon, who gently prodded me for years to capture these amazing stories. To Amanda, for your friendship and advice. To Valley Mamas, who walk beside me in the journey of motherhood. To my Rocktown Crossfit community, who holds me accountable to continually reach for my life goals. To Denny and Bonnie, for making me a part of your family. To Meredith, for your continued words of affirmation and encouragement when I needed them the most.

To everyone who listened to me talk about Grandmom, who also grew to love her as I do, thank you for sharing how much her story touched your hearts and inspiring me to write this book.

Made in the USA
Middletown, DE
12 October 2021